DO THE POSSIBLE WATCH GOD DO THE IMPOSSIBLE

Copyright 2016: Samuel Leeds
All rights reserved.
ISBN-13: 1530787944
Createspace
North Charleston, SC

LEGAL NOTICES

The information presented herein represents the view of the authors as of the date of publication. Because of the rate with which conditions change, the author reserves the right to alter and update his opinion based on the new conditions. This book is for informational purposes only. While every attempt has been made to verify the information provided in this book, neither the authors nor their affiliates/partners assume any responsibility for errors, inaccuracies or omissions. Any slights of people or organisations are unintentional. You should be aware of any laws which govern business transactions or other business practices in your country and state. Any reference to any person or business whether living or dead is purely coincidental.

Every effort has been made to accurately represent this product and its potential. Examples in these materials are not to be interpreted as a promise or guarantee of earnings. Earning potential is entirely dependent on the person using our product, ideas and techniques. We do not purport this as a "get rich scheme."

Your level of success in attaining the results claimed in our materials depends on the time you devote to the program, ideas and techniques mentioned your finances, knowledge and various skills. Since these factors differ according to individuals, we cannot guarantee your success or income level. Nor are we responsible for any of your actions.

Any and all forward looking statements here or on any of our sales material are intended to express our opinion of earnings potential. Many factors will be important in determining your actual results and no guarantees are made that you will achieve results similar to ours or anybody else's, in fact no guarantees are made that you will achieve any results from our ideas and techniques in our material.

ALL RIGHTS RESERVED. No part of this course may be reproduced or transmitted in any form whatsoever, electronic, or mechanical, including photocopying, recording, or by any informational storage or retrieval without the expressed written consent of the authors.

Do the Possible Watch God Do the Impossible

A practical guide to living a happy, rich and effective life taught through the Bible.

Samuel Leeds

Come to a Live Event and meet with other Christian business leaders at

WWW.TRAININGKINGS.CO.UK

About the author:

www.samuelleeds.org

TABLE OF CONTENTS

INTRODUCTION 9

Chapter 1: Find Your Calling 11

Chapter 2: Do the Possible,
          Watch God Do the Impossible 19

Chapter 3: Be Careful What You Think 29

Chapter 4: Know Your Strengths 39

Chapter 5: Get Wisdom 47

Chapter 6: Drop the Spiritual Baggage 55

Chapter 7: Be Content, Yet Ambitious 65

Chapter 8: Learn About Money 73

Chapter 9: Get Financially Free 87

Chapter 10: Run A Good Business 99

Chapter 11: Join A Network 115

Chapter 12: Live for Eternity 121

FINAL WORDS 130

ABOUT THE AUTHOR 131

INTRODUCTION

Congratulations on getting this book. Whether you are a Christian leader, a business owner or just somebody wanting to be more effective as a person, I believe as we journey together we can change culture for the better. The biblical philosophies found in this book have completely changed my life. Not just spiritually but financially, relationally, practically and productively.

I have spoken at countless Christian and business conferences and there is an awakening of people being released into their God-given calling and becoming Kingdom builders as they are impacting eternity.

In January 2014, I founded Training Kings which rapidly became the largest Christian business network in the UK. I am dearly proud of all the members as they bring their faith and business together and are making things happen for the Kingdom.

Lives are being changed, the poor are being supported and the good news of Jesus is increasing at a rate it has never before.

I want to invite you to be part of that and pray that as you read this book you will be inspired and equipped to walk as a royal priesthood through the mountains that God has mapped out for you.

By the time you finish the read, be prepared for your life to be on a completely different track.

Cheering you on all the way,

Samuel Leeds

CHAPTER 1:

Find Your Calling

So You Are A Christian, What Next?

As a teenager I went to a private Christian school but was always the one in trouble, getting into fights and continually on the edge on being expelled. My idea of being a Christian was being a weak and mild do-gooder and my idea of heaven was even worse. I did not want to go to a place with perfect people singing angelically for the whole of eternity to a God who was angry and distant. I just wanted to have as much fun as possible and not let anybody tell me what to do. I was a rebel and known as a thug in my bubble-wrapped private school. Upon leaving school I worked within my dad's business as an entertainer. I worked very hard, had little responsibility and was the king of my purposeless life.

Aged seventeen, I was lying in my bed ready to sleep but felt the presence of God in a way that I had never experienced before. My heart was beating fast and it was like God was sat right before me. He was neither angry nor disappointed. I was overwhelmed with a presence of love and every heartbeat was saying, "Jesus is alive." I found a bible and as I read it tears rolled down my cheeks. It was like reading a love story from God to man. The passages, stories and overall message became clear and as I accepted Jesus' love and forgiveness for me, my heart overflowed with love and forgiveness for others. It was a surreal experience and I have never been the same since. Thank God!

The next day I was faced with the big question, what next?

I knew that I wanted to live a different life. A life with purpose and meaning where I could feel God's presence all the time. I know there are many people in this boat. They are in a mundane job and feel their life has no purpose but have been born again and called for something bigger. They, like Jeremiah, have a fire shut up in their bones and in their heart that cannot be put out. Isaiah 58 talks about loosing chains of injustice, feeding the hungry, clothing the naked and sheltering the homeless. This is what I wanted to do, not work as an entertainer for dead end money.

So, that week, I quit my job and was ready for whatever God had in store for me. I decided to not eat while I searched for God's will. Yes, I was hardcore! I was in a state of "Here I am Lord". And after several days I heard...NOTHING! I was shocked as I thought that these kinds of fasts lead to seeing angels and everything. I tried other things, like going to prophetic conferences and getting up ridiculously early to pray. A few months went by before I heard...NOTHING!

Stop Looking For God's Will

The biggest myth in modern Christianity is that God works through mysterious signs and unclear confirmations. I was looking for God's will when I should have been looking for God. God is not superstitious and does not play games. He wanted me. It is quite remarkable that God wants to partner with us, not be our sat-nav.

"Do not conform to the pattern of this world, but be transformed by the renewing of your mind. Then you will be able to test and approve what God's will is-- his good, pleasing and perfect will." Romans 12:2 (this is the NIV version and I will be using this version of the bible for the duration of the book just for consistency)

We transform our mind by spending quality time with God and reading His word.

When you begin to develop an intimacy with Christ and understand God's character, you will see things in the world that need changing. You will see things as God sees them. I was looking for a booming voice from heaven to tell me..."Samuel, go to this place and do this!"

But now, my prayer is simply to see things as God sees them and have the courage to act. I don't spend six hours on my knees pressing in to hear God each morning, but do regularly ask,

"God, where are you going today? And can I come with you?"

Your Calling is What You See

We are all created differently and are called to do different things. God may partner with me on certain missions and you for others. But my question to you is, what do YOU see?

Maybe you see the starving children in some of the third world countries, or maybe you see those that go hungry in your own country. You may be burdened with the lost souls in this country, or maybe the fact that in some parts of the globe they have never even heard the Good News of Jesus. There are countless needs in this world. But I believe it is time to stop waiting around. Stop waiting for somebody to do something. Stop waiting to hear God's clear booming voice. You are the very people you have been waiting for. Your God-given calling is what you see. So many people are scared to do the wrong thing or step out in the wrong direction. This is fear talking not God. It is far better to take a step in the complete wrong direction than to not take a step at all. I would rather step out in the wrong direction, than not move at all. Reason being is that God will guide your steps if you are moving, but standing still is a dangerous place to be.

Let's take a look at Moses. Moses saw that the Israelites were being treated wrongly and it broke his heart. He fled and began to seek God, not God's will. God touched his heart and Moses knew that somebody had to do something about it - and that somebody was him. Moses was sure that he was not the right man for the job. He had a speech impediment and was way out of his depth. However, he obeyed God and went anyway because that was his calling. That was what he had seen.

Now, this principle applies to all aspects of your life and can be used on a regular basis. Some examples may be:

You see that your relationship with your spouse could be better.
You see that you need to lose weight.
You see a gap in the market place and an opportunity to make some money.
You see the same homeless man begging on the street and wish somebody would give him some food and sort him some shelter.
You think of a really good book that somebody should write.

STOP waiting! Just do it!
Transform your mind and do what you see.

Exercises

1. Spend some time reflecting on God's love for you and enjoy some quiet time with Him. Ask Him,

"God, where are you going? And can I come with you?"

2. Think about three things that you wish were different in the world or in your life.

-

-

-

3. Write down any opportunities that you have seen but not pursued because of fear.

CHAPTER 2:

Do the Possible, Watch God Do the Impossible

God Never Said It Would Be Easy

We all know the story of David and Goliath in the book of 1 Samuel. It is a story that is taught in Sunday school and glossed over as a 'nice story'. However, this historical account that has been God-breathed into scripture is actually packed with lessons about God and us that are absolutely life changing.

Goliath was a nine-foot tall, Philistine giant. He was a well-known fighting champion and had been a warrior since his youth. Goliath decided to demand a one-on-one fight with one of the Israelites and the winning team would rule the other nation. Not a fair deal whatsoever, as Goliath was clearly the best fighter going.

When people ask me,

"If God is alive and loving then why are there so many problems in the world and in my life?"

I find it quite bemusing, as God never promised you an easy life. God never said there would be no problems in the world. The bible is full of them. He did promise to walk with you as together you overcome those problems. The bible is filled with accounts of people overcoming problems whilst walking with the Lord.

Do Not Just Trust God

The Israelites became more and more terrified when Goliath would come and give his highly intimidating speech twice each day without fail.
David's older brothers were included but David himself had no idea what was going on. He was just a shepherd boy watching the flock in the distance. When David came one day to give his brothers some food he heard Goliath's speech. David's response was incredible.

In paraphrase, he said,

"Do not be afraid. Let us trust in God, who will prevail at the right time."

Is this Right?...NO!

David did not say that! In fact quite the opposite! This would have been a very spiritual thing to say that would have ticked all the Christian boxes. "Let's trust God." "If it's meant to be it will be." "When the going gets tough, trust God and let's duck!"

But David actually said, "Give me a sling shot and a stone and let me at him".

In 1 Samuel 17:34-38, David reports to King Saul,

"Your servant has been keeping his father's sheep. When a lion or a bear came and carried off a sheep from the flock, I went after it, struck it and rescued the sheep from its mouth. When it turned on me, I seized it by its hair, struck it and killed it. Your servant has killed both the lion and the bear; this uncircumcised Philistine will be like one of them, because he has defied the armies of the living God. The Lord who rescued me from the paw of the lion and the paw of the bear will rescue me from the hand of this Philistine."

In God's Strength or Yours?

This is often a disputed topic amongst theologians. Was David fighting Goliath in his own strength and using his own skills? Or was David just a shepherd boy moving in the power of God?
Some argue that David is an example of how to use your God-given strengths. He was a fine shepherd boy but also had trained himself in using a slingshot and how to fight animals.

1 Timothy 4:14 says,

"Do not neglect your gift…"

It was David's skill that brought down Goliath, not a supernatural intervention by God. In the same way, as a church we are a body and all have different gifts and should each use them accordingly for one good purpose. God is a practical God and wants us to use our practical skills.

Sounds fair enough right?

Though others argue that this is not the case at all and the first perspective is completely undermining to the power of God. They say that God loves to use the weak to show his glory and in this example David was just a shepherd boy and without God he had no chance of winning. This is a story to show how God can use ordinary people to do extraordinary things.

The bible says,

"My grace is sufficient for you, for my power is made perfect in weakness." Therefore (Paul goes on to say) I will boast all the more gladly about my weaknesses, so that Christ's power may rest on me. That is why, for Christ's sake, I delight in weaknesses, in insults, in hardships, in persecutions, in difficulties. For when I am weak, then I am strong." 2 Corinthians 12:9-11.

So the question is, does God want to see you go and use YOUR strengths to be effective in His Kingdom?

Or does God want you to solely rely on Him and deny all confidence in the flesh?
This is a very important question.

With this in minds, let us take a look at what David said. He began by telling stories of how capable and experienced he was in killing strong animals. He had a good track record and was clearly very skilled. He then closes with saying,
"The Lord who rescued me from the paw of the lion and the paw of the bear will rescue me from the hand of this Philistine."

David was not going alone, but he was going with God. He knew that he was able to work in partnership with God. Working in partnership with God is the key to being truly effective in His Kingdom.

It is something that needs to be deliberate and practised. The danger of going alone is that you will either lose or become arrogant in winning. God doesn't want either. The problem with not going at all is that God has called you to go. In the church we are quick to judge arrogance but slow to judge laziness and fear. Laziness and fear can often be masked with over-spiritual claptrap such as "I am waiting on the Lord to speak." When really you just don't have the confidence to take any action.

Partnering With God

If I had to explain this philosophy of working in partnership with God and what it looks like in one sentence, it would be,

"Do the possible, and watch God do the impossible."

David knew that he could not defeat Goliath on his own, but used his strengths to do all he could, while having faith God would do the rest. This is a perfect example of how we should be facing the giants in our life on a day-to-day basis.

Once you understand this, you will begin to see it all over the bible. There are countless stories of ordinary people doing all they can do, and then God showing up. God could have happily parted the red sea on His own, but He still asked Moses to raise his staff in order to make it happen.

Exodus 14:15-18
"Then the Lord said to Moses, "Why are you crying out to me? Tell the Israelites to move on. Raise your staff and stretch out your hand over the sea to divide the water so that the Israelites can go through the sea on dry ground. I will harden the hearts of the Egyptians so that they will go in after them. And I will gain glory through Pharaoh and all his army, through his chariots and his horsemen. The Egyptians will know that I am the Lord when I gain glory through Pharaoh, his chariots and his horsemen."

In the same way, when we come to God begging for a break through, He says,

"Why are you crying out to me?"

This is a real mind shift and often not our perspective of how we think God works but is blatantly obvious through all scripture. God wants you to go and He will then go with you. The glory will be His and you will be His partner. If you want the Holy Spirit to show up, stop praying for Him to come. When you go and do God's work, He will come!

There is an old saying,

"Do the thing and have the power."

Working in partnership with God is a humbling experience because He doesn't need us, but chooses to let us in. Part of the template is always that the result will bring glory to God.

You Will Face Opposition

I must warn you that when you begin to do the possible, these things will probably happen.

You will be falsely accused.
You will be undermined.
You will annoy the heck out of people.

This is normal and also happened to David. David's eldest brother "burned with anger" when he saw David getting involved with the battle. Don't sign up for the class that studies why people are annoyed. They just will be. Move on!

He was also falsely accused,

"I know how conceited you are and how wicked your heart is; you came down only to watch the battle."

David turned away. Do not get enticed into pointless arguments, walk away and get on with your mission.

King Saul told him,

"You are not able to go against this Philistine and fight him, you are only a young man and he has been a warrior from his youth."

Most people are fast to stop you before you get started, but hesitant to get in the way once you're moving.

In Conclusion

David beat Goliath, cut off his head and was crowned King by the very same people who had opposed him.

So, in chapter 1, you wrote down three things that you have seen that somebody needs to do something about.

David saw that somebody needed to defeat Goliath. He did the possible, and watched God do the impossible. For David, the possible was asking Saul to arrange the fight.

Now is time to ask yourselves, what is your possible? If the mission is way bigger than you, that is great. Next, go on to complete the exercises and watch what happens when you apply them.

Exercises

1. Meditate on these verses and state them out loud.

Romans 8:31
"If God is for us, who can be against us?"

Philippians 4:13
"I can do all things through Christ, who gives me strength."

2. Refer to the three things you wrote down in the first chapter, and now write down at least one practical thing you can do towards solving that problem.

-

-

-

CHAPTER 3
Be Careful What You Think

Positive Thinking

There are thousands of positive thinking books that you can read but most of them are flawed and I find them extremely irritating. The first says that life comes without hardships or troubles. It says that you can make anything happen through positive thinking and effectively you become your own god. The second book steals philosophies straight from the bible and makes them appear to be a new idea made up by them.

Biblical Positive Thinking

In this chapter, I want to look at what the bible says about positive thinking and how this can assist us to be highly effective.

There is one huge difference between those who are highly effective and those who just get by. The difference is what they think about. It would be wrong to assume that only you and God know what goes on inside your head. What you think about will always show through in your life and it is important to be aware of this.

If you were to think about a sad memory for instance, it would be naive to think that you would not begin to feel sad. In the same way, if you were to reminisce over a happy thought, it would have a positive effect on your feelings. So we can conclude that what you think about leads to how you feel.

How you feel then leads to what you do. If you feel lazy, the chances are you will not do much work. Whereas if you feel inspired, you will probably get something worthwhile done. Can you see the direct correlation between what you feel and what you do? If you feel hungry you will go and make a sandwich. If you feel sleepy you will go to bed. So if thoughts will lead to feelings and then your feelings will lead to actions, what you think about is pretty important right? Yes.

The miracle part is that your actions will then determine your life.

T Harv Eker, famously gives this formula:

Thoughts - Feelings - Actions = Your Life

To illustrate this formula, I will tell you about the time I invested in a treadmill only for it to become a large ornament in my home. My siblings and I were infamously known for requesting expensive kits for

Christmas such as a karate outfit, only to go once and then quit. If you are honest, you have probably done something similar.

So why do you think so many people know what they ought to do but just do not have the discipline to follow through? I know why and it is quite simple. It is because they don't FEEL like it. The reason you don't go on that run, make that important business call, attend that event or send those follow up emails, is because you don't feel like it.
Well imagine if you could change the way you feel through your thoughts? Would that make a big difference? Well you can!

This is an extremely well quoted verse in motivational talks and personal development seminars that says,

"As a man thinks, so he is."

I always thought this was first said by Napoleon Hill in the book 'Think and Grow Rich' but it is actually an ancient verse found in Proverbs 23:7.

T Harv Eker is well known for saying,

"What you focus on expands."

This is very true. If you are overweight and want to get fit, I would advise rather than morbidly looking in the mirror and weighing yourself each evening, instead picture yourself as a slim healthy person and then set out to become that person. Focus on all the advantages of being healthy and as you change the way you feel, your actions will follow. Ultimately your actions are what will change things but the foundations are set with right thinking.

Turn Your Back on the Problem

One of the Training Kings members came to me with £16,000 worth of bad debt and was earning less than he could live on. He would spend nights tossing and turning about his debt and thinking about how to pay it off. I told him to stop thinking about the debt, and start focusing on his business and how to create more income. Within less than a year he had paid off all of his debt without a worry in the world.

On this basis, if you want a better life then start fixing your eyes on the good and stop spending time looking at the bad because what you focus on really does expand.

I personally am not into cars but knew my wife, Amanda, was saving for an Audi sports car. I researched the model she wanted and bought it for her as a surprise just before our wedding. She was delighted. When giving her the car it was the first time I had seen that model. It was beautiful. From that day on I suddenly started spotting them everywhere. It was almost like the world had found out the car we had bought and decided to copy us or maybe I had just become a magnet to that car. The truth is that because I had spent so much time looking at the car, I was well acquainted with it and would now notice other cars the same. There were no more models made, but in my new world they were everywhere. My question to you - what do you spend time looking at and what have you become acquainted to?

You are a Magnet

I know many people who are bad news magnets. Everywhere they go, bad news seems to follow them. They have learned to expect it to the point that when things go right they subconsciously sabotage the good news and turn it to bad news! Remember the story of the Israelites after they had been freed from being slaves in Egypt. God told them to remember their exile and rejoice and they would enter the Promised Land. Instead they murmured about the food and heat and as a result died in the desert never entering the Promised Land.

On the other hand, there are those people who seem to be favoured in such a way that everything they touch turns to gold. Why is this? Because they have learned to focus and think about good things and that is exactly what manifests in their life. Try not to be a person of success, but be a person who attracts success.

Be an Overcomer

The story of Joseph is a superb example of how this works. Joseph was not unfamiliar with hardship, but he was an overcomer. Do not put your head in the sand and pretend that life never has challenges, but learn to focus on the good and be an overcomer of the bad. Despite being abandoned by his brothers, sold as a slave and unfairly thrown into prison, he always was a man of excellence and chose to live a pure and good life. This is the reason that everything he touched would turn to gold. Despite his difficulties he ended up being the prince of Egypt, uniting with his family and saving many lives across the nations. Joseph chose to be a positive and right thinker and this lead to his success, effectiveness and happiness.

Time to Throw Out the Television?

The bible says,

"Finally, brothers, whatever is true, whatever is honourable, whatever is just, whatever is pure, whatever is lovely, whatever is commendable, if there is any excellence, if there is anything worthy of praise, think about these things." Philippians 4:8

We are not doing God any favours by obeying this commandment. This is written for our own personal development and so we can be a happier, more effective person in the world. Be careful about letting trash be bombarded into your brain. I choose not to have a television and drastically limit how much News I will listen to. I have been rebuked by many and they say that I need to know what is going on in the world by spending every evening listening to bad news stories and hearing about the latest celebrity divorce. No thanks!

God has not created us to be addicted to listening to bad news for entertainment that desensitises our consciousness and numbs our minds. If it's that important, I will find out.

My mum used to always tell me to count my blessings. It seemed like a nice thing to do but I never realised the powerful effect this has on your life. What a beautiful habit to develop in the simplest form of positive thinking.

"Bless the LORD, O my soul, and forget not all of his benefits."
Psalm 103:2

The Eagle Story

There is a story about a mother eagle who lost one of her eggs. Of all places this egg had could have landed, it had fallen into a chicken coop. The mother chicken of the coop cared for the egg as her own and when the baby eagle was finally hatched it was thought it was a chicken.
This baby eagle would scratch around like a chicken, even eating chicken seed. He never tried to fly because in his mind he was just another chicken.

In this poor baby eagle's heart it desired to soar in the sky and be free, but all the other chickens thought he was silly and told him to stop dreaming. "You're just a chicken like us." They would say. One day this eagle tried to fly but as it got a few feet in the air the other chickens jumped up and pulled him to the floor. They were simply trying to protect their younger sibling thinking it would fall or die in the wild, not realising that he was destined to be free.

One day, when the baby eagle was in its coop, he saw his true mother soaring in the sky. He had not seen anything like it but immediately identified himself with this magnificent eagle and knew that this must be its true mum. As soon as this revelation became apparent, the baby eagle soared into the sky and joined his mum. The chickens were quick to stop him when planning, but would not try and get in his way when soaring.

Thoughts lead to feelings, these feelings lead to actions, which lead to how you live your life. When the baby eagle thought it was a chicken, it could not act like an eagle. In the same way, we are children of God. When we identify Him as our father and believe that we are a new creation, we will manifest different things. This is not mere positive thinking this is biblical thinking.

Exercise

Do not complain about ANYTHING or anyone for 24 hours.

List 50 things that you are grateful for in life and thank God for them...
"Every good or perfect gift is from above."
James 1:17

1
2
3
4
5
6
7
8
9
10
11
12
13
14
15
16
17
18
19
20
21
22
23
24
25
26

27
28
29
30
31
32
33
34
35
36
37
38
39
40
41
42
43
44
45
46
47
48
49
50

CHAPTER 4
Know Your Strengths

Don't Be Like The Rest

When I was at school I was pretty terrible at most subjects. My attention span was extremely short and I spent most of my time clock-watching until I would get to leave the stuffy classroom and enjoy delivering my paper rounds. There was one subject that I absolutely loved though, and that subject was Speakers Class. In Speakers Class we would have to memorise and put together speeches and then deliver them to the whole school and often visitors and parents included. I absolutely loved it.

It was a strange feeling being able to wipe the floor with all my smart classmates every single time. The girl who was always teachers pet and would get top marks in everything, suddenly found herself getting beaten by the kid who spent most days in detention. Everybody would stress over their lines and be nervous before their speech, whereas I would revel in it and always get top marks. I used to happily practise my speech at home and record myself whenever possible. My teachers advised me to spend more time revising my other subjects though, as I was 'already good at speaking'.

When it was time for me to pick my final subjects, I was informed that Speakers Class was no longer available so I had to give it up. I was very disappointed but was advised by all the mature working adults that in the 'real world' Maths and Geography were more important. It's funny that over 90% of what I learned in Maths I have now forgotten and even if I had remembered it, I am confident I would not have used it to this day. But being able to communicate and speak is where all my income comes from and I have learned more geography travelling the world speaking than I ever did in Geography class.

Isn't that interesting?

It was not long after leaving school when I started out in business - property investing. I had nothing to invest but was excellent at finding ways to buy property creatively. I bought my first house at eighteen years old and managed to finance it using none of my own money. The profit from just that first house was leaving me with an income of £1,000 per month.

It soon became apparent that I had a good business mind and was a natural entrepreneur so I went on to study Business at night school, which enabled me to continue growing the business in the day. While training I was continually warned about all the hardships of business and made to complete dozens of assignments. There was a never-ending amount of checklists, market research and admin type jobs to be done and I began to lose entrepreneurial flare.

Learn Your Strengths and Weaknesses

There seemed to be a pattern developing that started in school whereby the things that I loved doing would get swallowed up by the things that had to be done. This was not just the case for me but is true for pretty much everybody. Whether you are in school, running your own business or even in the corporate world. If you are in a job and your boss notices you are not too good at customer service, you will be sent on a 'Customer Service Training Course'. We are all taught to be well rounded, balanced individuals. Since then, I did a study on highly effective people and researched how they manage their skills and how they go about completing the tasks that they may not strive in. The results changed my life.

The people who change history by being outstanding in what they do, are not all-rounders nor are they balanced. Mohammed Ali was one of the greatest boxers of all time. He was not that good at Karate though. He didn't want to be an all-round fighter. He loved boxing, was a natural and spent all his time focusing on being a better boxer and that is why he was a champion.

Sir Richard Branson is an extremely successful entrepreneur and his business, Virgin, is arguably the best business set up in the whole of the UK. However, until only a few years ago he would get confused about the difference between gross and net profit. I know this is true because I have heard him tell the story personally. How could he get so confused over such a basic finance definition? Because he knows his strengths. Sir Richard Branson is an outstanding creator and delegator. He doesn't want to be an all-round balanced businessman but chooses to play to his strengths and push that for all he is worth. That is why Sir Richard Branson is so effective and successful.

List as many strengths you can think of. The things you love doing. The things you are naturally excellent at. (Ignore the action points at this point.)

Strengths: Action Points:

-
-
-
-
-
-
-
-

List as many weaknesses you can think of. The things you dread doing.
Ask your close friends and family to help. (Ignore the action points at this point.)

Weaknesses: Action Points:

-
-
-
-
-
-
-
-

By this point you should have a list of strengths and weaknesses. The big question now is, what are you going to do about them?

Dealing with Your Weaknesses

There are three things you should do with your weaknesses.

Scrap doing it. Outsource it. Partner with somebody who loves doing it.

I spoke with a business owner called John recently. John works within IT and hates cold calling prospects. This is where you have to make phone calls to strangers, trying to sell your products and services. It is an aspect to John's business that he knows he has to do, but every week it hangs over him like a dark black cloud. He loves looking after existing customers and managing all the computers. He even loves taking new enquiries and going networking. But the rejection he gets from selling and initiating unwanted calls makes him sick.

I asked him,

"John, how much time do you spend cold calling per week?"

He responded,

"Maybe 30 minutes each day."

I asked him to track exactly how much time he spends cold calling in a journal and come back to me the following week. To his surprise he actually only spent a grand total of seventy-five minutes that week cold calling but probably around seven hours thinking about it.

Surely, John needs to go on a class where they teach him to not fear cold calling? Or maybe I should just give him some advice on how to do it better? Absolutely not! Instead, I told John to never make a cold call again. Ever! He was shocked and seemed a little worried so decided to start by trying it for a month. For one whole month, he would not make a single cold call. At the end of that month his sales had gone through the roof and business was better than ever. He was also happier than usual. Previously, he had been so worried about cold calling that he was awful at it and never made sales doing it anyway. The only effect it had on him was to distract him from other things and make him generally unproductive.

What lessons can you learn from this? Are there things in your life that actually do not need to be done? Well it is time to scrap them then. There may be some instances where you may not be able to scrap them. You may have to outsource it out instead. For instance, when my phone used to ring, I used to answer it myself. Not anymore! I have a PA who deals with all my calls when I am busy as well as all my emails. It is important to outsource all the things that you are not needed for.

If you have not got the finance to outsource everything, there may be some things that you can partner people into. If you want to put on a big conference and have all the abilities to make it a great day, but are not so good at getting bums on seats, why not partner with somebody who can fill in the gaps that you are not so good at.

So, go back to the list of all your weaknesses and write under the Action Points what your plan is to do with them.

Will you scrap it, outsource it or partner on it?

Utilising Your Strengths

Following this you need to know what to do with your strengths. Please do these two things.

Train yourself to be even better. Fill your diary with these strengths.

When I discovered this "Know your strengths" philosophy, I put speaking as one of my top strengths. I then looked through my diary and had around only three speaking engagements that month! I decided to fill my diary with them, joined speaking associations and began to read books on the subject. If you are naturally good at something and also immerse yourself in that field you will become outstanding. I would rather be outstanding at one thing than average at several.

So, go back to the list of all your strengths and write under the Action Points how you plan to maximise them into your business and personal life.

CHAPTER 5
Get Wisdom

If God gave you one wish, what would you ask for?

We read in the bible how Solomon asked for wisdom. Let's take a look at this as there are many great lessons to be learned.

2 Chronicles 1:1-13

"Solomon went up to the bronze altar before the Lord in the tent of meeting and offered a thousand burnt offerings on it. That night God appeared to Solomon and said to him, "Ask for whatever you want me to give you." Solomon answered God, "You have shown great kindness to David my father and have made me king in his place. Now, Lord God, let your promise to my father David be confirmed, for you have made me king over a people who are as numerous as the dust of the earth. Give me wisdom and knowledge, that I may lead this people, for who is able to govern this great people of yours?" God said to Solomon, "Since this is your heart's desire

and you have not asked for wealth, possessions or honour, nor for the death of your enemies and since you have not asked for a long life but for wisdom and knowledge to govern my people over whom I have made you king, therefore wisdom and knowledge will be given you. And I will also give you wealth, possessions and honour, such as no king who was before you ever had and none after you will have."
Then Solomon went to Jerusalem from the high place at Gibeon, from before the tent of meeting, to Jerusalem. And he reigned over Israel."

What is wisdom?

Wisdom is the application of knowledge. It is interesting to note that Solomon did not ask God to bless the people or provide for the needy. He asked God to give him something, wisdom. This was not a selfish request because the outcome was for the good of the people. There is nothing wrong with wanting to accumulate knowledge or wealth as long as your heart is right and your thinking goes beyond yourself. It is possible that your biggest gift to the world is your own personal development and that is why God commended Solomon for requesting wisdom and knowledge.

If you chase after money, you are chasing the wrong thing. When a poor person wins the lottery they usually end up in the exact same financial position within a couple of years. Similarly, if you were to take all the riches from a millionaire, chances are within two years they would be a millionaire again. This is because wisdom is far more important than money. If you have the knowledge to make millions of pounds, that is far greater than having the millions of pounds. That is why we read,

"How much better to get wisdom than gold, to get insight rather than silver!" (Proverbs 16:16)

Wisdom is not just the ability to make money. That may be one example of an aspect to wisdom, but wisdom is being able to apply knowledge. This spills out into many different aspects of life, but if you have wisdom do not be surprised when people travel miles just to come and tap into your understanding.

Albert Einstein said,

"Try not to be a person of success, but a person of value."

If you are a person of value and great wisdom, the success will follow however that looks for you. That is why Jesus says,

"But seek first His kingdom and His righteousness, and all these things will be given to you as well." Matthew 6:33

Therefore, get wisdom, get understanding. Next question, how?

How do we get wisdom?

1. Acknowledge your Maker

Proverbs 9:10 says,

"The fear of the Lord is the beginning of wisdom."

This is not being scared of God but acknowledging Him in His true sense. The more we learn about God the more in awe we become, which is a healthy fear and respect, the kind a child has for their father. Without knowing God, you cannot be truly wise because He is the meaning of life. Without having an understanding of eternity, any earthly wisdom is in vain. So the first step towards getting wisdom is to begin to know and understand God, the giver of wisdom.

2. Ask God

God has promised us a remarkable thing.

"If any of you lacks wisdom, you should ask God, who gives generously to all without finding fault, and it will be given to you." James 1:5.

What an incredible offer! So the same wisdom that was given to King Solomon is accessible to us all, when we simply ask. If you haven't already asked, now is the time.

3. Listen to the wise

Research shows that we are the makeup of the five people we spend the most time with. Who do you hang around with? Well, I can confidently say that you will be very similar to them. Your wealth, your language, your ethics, your goals and your wisdom. Maybe you are thinking of making some new friends after hearing this? Well, that may be a good idea but you can spend time with people without having to physically be with them. I have had many mentors that I have never met with in person but I have found my character and thinking changing while reading their books and biographies or listening to their audio CD's. For the rest of this chapter, we will be tapping into some of Solomon's wisdom and taking on board his inspired mentoring from the verse,

"Go to the ant, you sluggard; consider its ways and be wise!"
Proverbs 6:6.

Observe the Ant

If the wisest man who ever lived, Solomon, advises us to consider the ways of the ant, then I suggest we should do it. I myself, with some help from Jim Rohn, have done a study on ants and will be concluding the top three lessons I found, which have gone on to serve me well.

1. Ants never quit.

If an ant is on a journey only to be blocked by a wall, it will go around the wall. If it cannot get around it, it will go the other way. If that fails it will begin to climb over the wall. Only after becoming clear that it is impossible to get over the wall, will the ant begin to dig under the wall. Finally, if all else fails, the ant will relentlessly dig through the wall. The ant does not quit!

The only time to quit something good is to replace it with something great. Many people will try and persuade you to quit and give you other ideas and projects to work on. Do not be swayed by the wind. Once you have been assigned your God-given mission, do not quit! It is normal to feel like quitting sometimes but be like the ant and relentlessly find a way to make it happen. Join Jim Rohn and be able to say,

"This is my mountain and I am getting to the top. You are either going to see me dead at the side or waving from the top because I am not going back!"

2. Ants work together

An ant on its own is pretty insignificant. Ants working together can move rocks. If you want to see teamwork in its most brilliant sense then search on Youtube for 'ants working together' and you'll be amazed as to the magnificent teamwork that happens amongst ants. Each ant has its own specific role but they have one mission. Like ants, humans are pretty insignificant too, when alone, but when two or three together agree on a common purpose then nothing can stop them.

Next, the ant does not say,

"What can the others do for me?"
But rather,
"What can I do for others?"

In the same way, we should always ask what we can give, not what can we get. Don't ask what your country can do for you, but ask what you can do for your country. Don't ask what your church can do for you, but what can you do for your church. This philosophy is applicable to all of life, even in a marriage. If people went into marriage to give, there would not be a 50% chance of divorce. It would probably be closer to 0%.

3. Ants think ahead

In the summer when everybody else is resting, the ant is preparing for the winter. In the winter when everybody is working and moaning in the cold, the ant knows that the summer is on its way.

When you are in the dry seasons and the clouds are heavy, can you see the ray of sunlight shining through the clouds? When you are in the valleys, can you lift your eyes to the hills and know that summer is on the way?

Alternatively, when things are prospering, have you the wisdom to put aside a percentage for the winter seasons? When life is rosy, have you the compassion to mourn with a suffering friend?

When Joseph was the Prince of Egypt, he had the wisdom to put aside one-seventh of the nations wealth for when there would be famine. This is how the ant thinks too. Ants work hard but they also work smart.

If you work hard and smart with a never quitting mentality while working in a team, you will change history.

As you can see, there is much merit in observing the ant and I hope you continue this study in your quest to be a wiser and more effective person.

Exercises

Who are the top five people that you spend the most time with?

-
-
-
-
-

Are you happy with being like them?

CHAPTER 6
Drop the Spiritual Baggage

Do not separate the secular and the divine

A great misconception amongst many Christians is that there is a divide between the secular and the spiritual. Spiritual things include church, prayer meetings, Christian songs, mission trips, evangelism and reading the bible. Secular things are those that have nothing to do with God. These may include going to work, socialising with 'non-christian' friends, going to amusement parks or just driving the car, unless in the car you were listening to worship music of course.

This thinking is not only incorrect but will also lead you to being a highly ineffective Christian. You will end up feeling guilty about not doing enough for God, and at the same time not enjoy normal life.

In contrast to this incorrect thinking of separating the secular and the divine, the bible says that the earth is the Lord's and everything in it. This means that everything is spiritual. You cannot put God into a box nor your faith. Godfrey Birtill wrote a song called "Are You Ready?" and the lyrics say,

"Glory in the kitchen, glory in the hall,
Glory in the living room, dining room and all.
Glory in the bathroom, angels sing,
Glory in the bedroom, sweet sleeping.
Glory in the garage, glory in the lounge,
The glory of the Lord's all over the house.
Glory in the restaurant, glory in the pub,
Glory in prison, glory in the club.
Glory in the shops, glory in the park,
Glory in the bank and the cinema.
Glory in the dentists checking out your teeth.
The glory of the Lord is falling in the streets.
Glory on the bus, glory on the train,
Glory in the car, glory on the plane.
Glory when I run, glory when I hike,
Glory when I swim, glory on my bike.
Glory going to play, glory going to work.
The glory of the Lord is covering the earth."

If you are in a 'secular' job and feeling frustrated about not working in full-time ministry, perhaps you need to realise that your full-time ministry is simply glorifying God in everything you do, including your job. God has called us to be all in different places doing different things and He does not want a world full of preachers and overseas missionaries.

"So whether you eat or drink or whatever you do, do it all for the glory of God." 1 Corinthians 10:31.

Doing something for the glory of God does not mean shouting "Hallelujah" at as many opportunities as possible. To glorify means to 'magnify'. So glorifying God is living in such a way that magnifies Him. In all you say and do, let people see the beauty of Jesus in you, that He may be known. It is often not appropriate to tell the full gospel to everybody you meet all the time. When you are at work, you may be working with a customer or a colleague, you are not being paid to preach the gospel, you are being paid to work. However, if you are carrying the presence of Jesus and working in an excellent way that magnifies Him, you will give people a glimpse of the diamond, namely Jesus. People will ask you to explain your faith when they see it. That is what we read in 1 Peter 3:5,

"Always be prepared to give an answer to everyone who asks you to give the reason for the hope that you have. But do this with gentleness and respect."

Peter assumes that you will be living in such a way that people do ask you, "What is so different about you?", "Where does your hope come from?" or "Why are you so happy all the time?"

To not answer them would be rude. You can then tell them about how Jesus found you and has given you a new life. This conversation could happen anywhere. This is an example of how God is in all things and why you should never separate the divine and the secular.

Gifts, not duties

God has not burdened us with rules and duties, but instead transforms us into new creations and blesses us with more gifts than we can count. I find it curious that people think that they are earning brownie points by keeping God's commandments. When we are walking in God's Kingdom as heirs of Christ, there are certain boundaries that we do not cross and there are rules we are given. However, this is not for God but actually a gift for us.

Let's look at four key habits that may appear to be difficult burdens but in fact are wonderful gifts.

1. Keep the Sabbath Holy

"Remember the Sabbath day by keeping it holy. Six days you shall labour and do all your work, but the seventh day is a sabbath to the Lord your God. On it you shall not do any work, neither you, nor your son or daughter, nor your male or female servant, nor your animals, nor any foreigner residing in your towns. For in six days the Lord made the heavens and the earth, the sea, and all that is in them, but he rested on the seventh day. Therefore the Lord blessed the Sabbath day and made it holy." Exodus 20:8-11.

I know people that say they are too busy to have one whole day off each week, and they pretty much work

24/7. They get more work done to begin with, but they begin to lose touch with their family and friends and their relationship with God runs dry very quickly. After a year or two they begin to get extremely stressed and after three years have a nervous breakdown. This puts them out of action completely for two months while they recover. If they go back to the old way of working, it will not be long before they have a heart attack and have to have even longer time off work to recover. All the while having no meaningful relationship with God or their family.

Can you see that this is an unproductive and extremely short-sighted way to live? God has given us the blueprint of a six-day workweek as a gift, not a duty. If we choose to ignore Him there will be natural consequences, not because He is punishing us but because we are punishing ourselves. We are designed to have a day of rest each week. God Himself has even kindly demonstrated this template when He created the world. He also demonstrated this through His son, again as a gift. Keeping the Sabbath is not a duty given to burden us, but a gift from God for our good and to help us be highly effective.

2. Pray at all times

"And pray in the Spirit on all occasions with all kinds of prayers and requests. With this in mind, be alert and always keep on praying for all the Lord's people." Ephesians 6:18.

We are told many times to be continually praying.

"Rejoice always, pray continually, give thanks in all circumstances; for this is God's will for you in Christ Jesus." 1 Thessalonians 5:16-18.

It is so easy to think that because God has instructed us to always pray, that this is for His gain. This thinking is offensive to me and to God. To think that God wants us to pray because it makes Him feel good or He is lonely and in some way needs our prayers, is ludicrous. Prayer is a gift from God, not a duty.

When I was seven years old, I was really struggling with my maths. I would sit in front of my homework completely blank not understanding the question, let alone being able to answer it. Every Wednesday, my grandparents would come over and my granddad always told me,

"I want to see you do well and am proud of you working so hard on your maths. I am only in the other room, please call me anytime you like and I am happy to come and answer your questions."

I would sometimes feel bad about calling him so often, but he insisted it was ok and really helped me through that hard season of my life and I loved him all the more for it.

Question - did my Grandad get anything from me asking for his help?
Answer - No!

In the same way, God is always there and wants to assist you in all you do. When we pray, things happen and God moves. This is an absolute delight, not a burden.

Some prayers are not requests but thanksgiving. Again, this is not for God's ego. When we pray and thank God for our blessings, we change for the better. Remember in chapter 3, what we focus on expands.

So please do not feel guilty about lack of prayer, but take God up on his kind offer and embrace this awesome invite to partner and communicate with the Most High.

3. Love God and people

Mark 12:28-34

"One of the teachers of the law came and heard them debating. Noticing that Jesus had given them a good answer, he asked him, "Of all the commandments, which is the most important?"

"The most important one," answered Jesus, "is this: 'Hear, O Israel: The Lord our God, the Lord is one. Love the Lord your God with all your heart and with all your soul and with all your mind and with all your strength.' The second is this: 'Love your neighbour as yourself.' There is no commandment greater than these."

"Well said, teacher," the man replied. "You are right in saying that God is one and there is no other but him. To love him with all your heart, with all your understanding and with all your strength, and to love your neighbour as yourself is more important than all burnt offerings and sacrifices."

When Jesus saw that he had answered wisely, he said to him, "You are not far from the kingdom of God." And from then on no one dared ask him any more questions."

The number one commandment, loving God and loving people, is what all the other commandments hang upon.

We were all created with a desire to love and be loved. God wants us to be happy and wants to fulfil all of our deepest desires. Although this is a commandment, it is also a sheer joy. Like the rest of the commandments that stem from this. John Piper describes himself as a Christian Hedonist, meaning that he comes to God as a pleasure seeker. He believes that "God is most glorified in you, when you are most satisfied in Him." It is quite liberating to know that God's rules are given for our good. We are not bound by the law but through Christ we are free to keep the law.

In conclusion, drop all the spiritual baggage that ties you up in knots trying to please God and be a better Christian, and embrace your freedom in Christ. Glorify God in all you do and enjoy Him forever as you become an effective happy person.

Exercises

Read through the 10 Commandments but rather than trying harder to keep them, thank God that you are free to keep them as a new creation.

1. Thank you Lord that you have given me a heart that loves you and others.

2. Thank you Lord that I do not need to have any other gods, because you complete me.

3. Thank you Lord for the sweet name of Jesus.

4. Thank you Lord for giving me the Sabbath day to focus on you where I do not have to work.

5. Thank you Lord for my parents who raised me or brought me here.

6. Thank you Lord for giving me a forgiving heart that does not hate even my enemies.

7. Thank you for freeing me from an adulterous heart.

8. Thank you for giving me all I need and taking away any desire to steal.

9. Thank you for unloosing my tongue from one that tells lies, and giving me no reason to say anything apart from the truth.

10. Thank you for freeing me from envy and giving me all I need.

Meditate on Psalm 119.

"The law of the LORD is perfect, refreshing the soul. The statutes of the LORD are trustworthy, making wise the simple." vs 7.

"Oh, how I love your law! I meditate on it all day long." vs 97.

"How sweet are your words to my taste, sweeter than honey to my mouth!" vs 103.

CHAPTER 7
Be Content, Yet Ambitious

Resting in Jesus

When I first became a Christian at seventeen years old I was like a kid in a candy shop. I loved Gods presence so much and would fill my diary with just about every church event possible. This hunger for God had me travelling the world to experience what He was doing in other nations and I spent hours at a time in prayer, pressing in for more of God.

The bible says,

"Seek and you will find." Luke 11:9.

I was determined to keep seeking and find more.

All this searching and pressing in, began to get quite tiring, but I knew that this was just the battle of a believer. All good Christians had to soldier on, right?

While listening to some worship music on Youtube one evening, I heard a song by Godfrey Birtill with a beautiful peaceful melody and the lyrics are spoken as from God saying,

"There is no need to press in
When I'm already here
No point in wearing yourself out
On a treadmill of prayer.
Be still, Be still, Be still, Be still
Just be still and know
Your efforts aren't necessary
My work is 'believe'
Just be still and know
This rest is your testimony
My work you will see
Be still, Be still, Be still, Be still.
Living in the unforced rhythms of grace
Living in the unforced rhythms of grace
There is no need to draw close
When you're already in
No point in pushing labouring
Giving birth just to wind.
It's time to quit trying to please me
Quit trying to please me
Quit trying to please me,
Stop beating yourself up.
My heart is full of love for you!"

The music and lyrics touched my heart but I was wondering how that fit with all I had learned and read in the bible. What about the spiritual battle we are fighting? What about carrying our cross? What about seeking after God?

I began studying the bible again and had a new revelation. Up until this point, when reading the bible I had only been focussing on half of what I was reading. For example,

"Ask and it will be given to you; seek and you will find; knock and the door will be opened to you." Matthew 7:7.

I was only reading,

"Ask, ask, ask. Seek, seek, seek. Knock, knock and knock!"

During this revelation, rather than looking at what I was required to do, I began seeing what God had already done and believing in His promises. Maybe I was missing the point before? When the disciples came to Jesus and asked what was required of them to do, Jesus answered,

"The work of God is this: to believe in the one he has sent." John 6:29.

Jesus is the bread of life and when we come to Him we are made completely satisfied, no longer orphan children but complete in Him. Jesus says that He has come that "our joy may be complete". He says that if we are thirsty and come to Him we will "never thirst again."

Many say that we must suffer in order to be like Jesus. But the bible says,

"by His stripes, we are healed." Isaiah 53:5.

Jesus did not come to be our example but to take away the sins of the world by giving His life as a sacrifice.

When I began to walk in this freedom and no longer strive, some of my church friends saw this as 'backsliding'. I began to stop going to some of the boring meetings and saw through the pointless conferences for religions sake and instead enjoyed union with Christ. Everything I did was now driven by love for God and love for people, not to score brownie points. I wasn't getting into heaven from my works anyway, so why not just fully embrace the finished work of the cross?

Although I was now content which was great, would this new lifestyle of 'resting in Christ' make me ineffective? Would I no longer be ambitious because I am complete? Absolutely not! I began to dream bigger than ever before. Just because I was no longer ambitious to restore my relationship with God, this had already been done through Christ, I was even more ambitious to spread this Good News message and build His Kingdom.

The best way to motivate somebody is to get them to believe in the vision, not to dangle carrots and give them brownie points. When we stop messing around trying to save own own souls and accept that Jesus has already done this for us, we can then enjoy helping save others souls and moving onto bigger things.

Running the Race

There is a tension between being content and being ambitious.

The Apostle Paul said,

"I press on toward the goal to win the prize for which God has called me heavenward in Christ Jesus." Philippians 3:14.

Elsewhere he says,

"Therefore I do not run like someone running aimlessly; I do not fight like a boxer beating the air. No, I strike a blow to my body and make it my slave so that after I have preached to others, I myself will not be disqualified for the prize." 1 Corinthians 9:27.

This guy was hardcore! With this dogged determination and focused ambition, Paul almost single handedly spread the Christian message all across the world and took the church from a handful of people in Israel to hundreds and hundreds of thousands across the world. Paul would breeze through ship wrecks, carry on walking after being almost stoned to death and power sing his way out of prisons. He was described by many as a lunatic and known for being one of the most zealous men who ever lived. To say that Paul was ambitious would be the understatement of the century.

Yet in the very same letter, where he was talking about pressing on toward the goal, he says this,

"I have learned the secret of being content in any and every situation." Philippians 4:12.

Jesus also tells us to not worry about a thing, but trust in our Father to provide. Is this a contradiction from the highly ambitious verses? No!

Paul was ambitious, yet content. This is a remarkably powerful place to be in.

You may be sick of your job and mediocre life and want to go on to do something far greater. Some people will tell you to be content with what God has given you, but you need to be able to say,

"I have learned to be content with what I have, yet ambitious for more."

Perhaps you are in business and you want to take things to the next level and double your turnover. God wants you to be ambitious and have a "whatever it takes" mentality. But remember to be content with what you have also. This may sound like a contradiction but when you learn the art of balancing the two, you will become a massively more effective and happy person.

Exercises

1. Unless your motivation is purely down to love, quit all the religious activities you are involved with.

2. Read the book of Romans and Hebrews and meditate on the finished work of the cross.

3. Set some Kingdom goals and map out how you can make them happen, in partnership with God.

CHAPTER 8
Learn About Money

The church generally does not like to talk too much about money. The ones that do usually have twisted concepts rooted with emotional baggage linked with either fear or greed. It is ironic because the bible talks about money all the time. There are over 800 references about money throughout the bible.

There tends to be two perspectives on money amongst Christians, which are both horribly wrong. One is a poverty mindset and the other teaches prosperity nonsense.

Poverty Mindset

If you fall into this category you are probably good hearted but are held back by this incorrect thinking. You will likely sabotage any success that comes your way and feel guilty about making good money. You may also feel pulled between business success and fruitful ministry, forgetting that there is no divide between the secular and the divine.

You may think money is dirty and replace the word with things like "resource", "finance" or "seed".

You have always been told that it is greedy to earn more than you need. Sounds very humble doesn't it? Have you ever considered that if you have the capacity to earn more but choose not to, that is arguably selfish and almost certainly lazy?

Let's look at what the bible says about money and bust some of the misconceptions that we have been led to believe.

1. Money is the root of evil

"For the love of money is a root of all kinds of evil. Some people, eager for money, have wandered from the faith and pierced themselves with many griefs." 1 Timothy 6:10.

Let's be clear, that the money itself is not the issue here, but it is the "love of money." This was written originally in ancient Greek and the word used for "love of money" was just one word called "philarguria, φιλαργυρία". This word means to have an extreme greed for more money and is linked with covetous.

Do not fool yourself, money is neither good nor bad but is simply a tool that can be used for either. If you are envious of another person's ministry, that does not make the ministry evil, but your envy and greed is. In the same way, to demonise money is irrational.

If you elevate any good thing above God then you will run into problems. We are warned here to not value the gift above the giver. This is not condemning the gift. Money is a great resource and the concept of money came from God.

2. Rich people are less likely to enter into heaven

This is just nonsense and completely untrue. Some rich people are greedy but so are some poor people. Many of the hospitals, schools, churches and great christian ministries that stand today, only exist because wealthy Christians have supported them and helped establish them.

"Again I tell you, it is easier for a camel to go through the eye of a needle than for someone who is rich to enter the kingdom of God." Matthew 19:24.

This is another well-quoted verse from poverty minded Christians who fail to remember the next part of the scripture.

"When the disciples heard this, they were greatly astonished and asked, "Who then can be saved?" Jesus looked at them and said, "With man this is impossible, but with God all things are possible."" Matthew 19:25, 26.

Jesus was not condemning the rich but was continually trying to show people that they cannot work their way into heaven. In context of the times, most people thought that being rich must mean that you are blessed and are going to heaven. That's why the disciples responded so surprised when Jesus said they had no chance. He was illustrating that it is impossible for absolutely anybody to get to heaven from his or her own merit, including the rich, and the only way was through Him. This verse has absolutely nothing to do with rich people being bad or greedy, nor should it deter you from wanting to make lots of money.

3. You have to choose; God or Money?

"No one can serve two masters. Either you will hate the one and love the other, or you will be devoted to the one and despise the other. You cannot serve both God and money." Matthew 6:24.

This is not saying that you have to choose whether to have God or money, you can have both! Let's take the verse into context with Luke 14:26,

"If anyone comes to me and does not hate his own father and mother, wife and children, brothers and sisters, yes, even their own life, such a person cannot be my disciple."

I don't know anybody that is scared of loving their family too much, but I meet hundreds of Christians scared of loving money too much. What these verses are saying is that we must have God on the throne. He is the giver of all these wonderful gifts, so to delight in the gifts but fail to acknowledge Him, is a gross sin. We should hate them only in comparison with Him. Of course we should love our family, Ephesians says we should love our wives like Christ loves the church. It is so important to not hang your whole theology on one verse taken out of context. You should translate that one verse though the whole bible, not the whole bible through one verse.

The conclusion we can draw from Matthew 6:24 is that money is a terrible master. However, taking the bible as a whole we know that money is a great servant. You cannot serve God and money but you can serve God through money.

4. Blessed are the poor

"Blessed are the poor in spirit, for theirs is the kingdom of heaven." Matthew 5:3.

The myth here is that if you are poor financially you are blessed, but if you are rich then you are greedy and will have to wait for your turn of misery. However, this verse is clearly not even talking about money. It says "the poor in spirit". The poor in spirit could include extremely rich business people who have a poor spirit and need Jesus more than ever. Be careful not to make the bible say what you want it to say.

I do believe that the poor financially will be blessed also, because God is a God of compassion and Jesus spent much time helping the poor. But to sabotage your success and desire to have no money in order to be blessed, would be warped and not how God created you to live.

5. The myth behind 'the rich young ruler'

There was a rich young ruler who wanted to know how he could be saved. Jesus' conclusion to him was,

"If you want to be perfect, go, sell your possessions and give to the poor, and you will have treasure in heaven. Then come, follow me."
When the young man heard this, he went away sad, because he had great wealth."

The first myth is that Jesus said he had to give 'everything' to the poor, when in fact Jesus never stated how much. The money was not the real issue anyway, it was not about selling his possessions, but as Jesus concluded it was, "then come, follow me.'

What Jesus was really saying was,

"Stop holding your money and possessions so tightly, but come and hold on to me."

It is also interesting to note, that this was not the first time Jesus had been asked this very same question - "What shall I do to be saved?" Surprisingly, Jesus always gave a completely different answer.
He told Nicodemus - you must be born again.
He told the Samarian woman - you must drink the water that I give.
He told the disciples - you must believe in the one God has sent.
He told the by-standers - you must eat my flesh and drink my blood.

Why would Jesus be so confusing? What was He trying to do? Jesus was giving them an answer that seemed impossible to them. His hope would be that the listener would give up hope in themselves, and realise they needed a Saviour. This would be the only way they would find true salvation because nobody can get into heaven through their own works.

The rich young ruler was missing one thing. He put money before God.
Jesus knew that was his problem and hit him where it hurt. He loved the man and wanted him to stop serving such a terrible master. He wanted the man to come and walk with him instead, but the man refused. If you hold your money with open hands and know that it belongs ultimately to God, you will be blessed. If you hold it with a tight first, it will hurt when God pulls open your fingers and this is what happened to the rich young ruler.

Prosperity Nonsense

If you are of the other extreme that believes that it is your right to be rich, I am sorry to tell you that your rights have been given up when you came to Jesus. Having money will not make you happy and there are more important things in life to worry about than driving a luxury car. If you were stripped naked and left homeless with not a penny in your pocket, would you be just as content as you are today? If the answer is no, then you need to question your heart. Let's look at some of the prosperity myths that are actually holding people back.

1. Money shows favour

"If they obey and serve him, they shall spend their days in prosperity, and their years in pleasures." Job 36:11.

Pulling a random verse from the bible that you happen to agree with and then hanging it on your office wall is never a good idea. Although there may be some truth in this verse please look at the context. This was something said to Job by Elihu, one of Job's advisers. There are mixed feelings about Elihu from theologians, some think he is a picture of Jesus and others think he is a jerk. Despite how you feel about this verse, many of Job's advisers were later in the book rebuked by God for their ridiculous advice. The above scripture was not God's voice.

Having no money has nothing to do with how holy you are. There is zero correlation between your financial wealth and your spiritual journey.
I know rich people who live sinful lives, just as I know poor people who live sinful lives. Similarly, I know rich people who are walking faithfully with the Lord, and I know poor people who are walking faithfully with the Lord.

The scary part is that some of these rich prosperity teachers go out to third world counties and preach this nonsense and it ends up in tears. The people elevate the preacher and put them on a pedestal only to end up feeling guilty that they cannot get out of poverty. This is heart breaking and happens due to an incorrect mindset about money.

2. Solomon was rich so you should be too

Yes, Solomon was a blessed man of God, but he was not perfect and had many flaws. Many prosperity teachers list rich people in the bible as though that means they ought to be rich too. Well, it doesn't.

These same people are desperate to prove that Jesus was also rich. There is much speculation around this but the bottom line is that it really doesn't matter how much money Jesus had and I am not going to bother giving my opinion on the matter.

God has no issues with you being rich, but he also will not intervene if you are determined to stay broke. There is no reason to justify anything as long as you are faithful with what you have and put God first in your life. I personally prefer to be wealthy but I know that my ultimate source of joy is in Jesus Christ. Someone once said,

"I have tried being broke. I didn't like it."

This is said in jest, but in all seriousness if you can live well, do it! But make sure God is number one and you are content with Him alone if needs be.

3. Ask anything and it will be given

"And I will do whatever you ask in my name, so that the Father may be glorified in the Son. You may ask me for anything in my name, and I will do it. If you love me, keep my commands. And I will ask the Father, and he will give you another advocate to help you and be with you forever" John 14:13-16.

This does not mean that as long as you put "In Jesus Name" at the end of any request that God is obliged to do it. Firstly, the promise in this verse, is protected, in that it has to be something that will glorify God. This may well be a personal request because God does receive glory when you are blessed, but do not expect God to grant self-centred or ego-driven prayers.

Secondly, there are no time restrictions here. I am not watering down the promise, and I do believe that God is often immediate, but sometimes our plans and timeframes, are different to His.

Thirdly, there is an assumption that you love God and are walking in accordance with His commandments. If you have no relationship with God, your prayers are just words.

Lastly, Jesus says that in answering your prayer, He will ask the Father to send another advocate to help you. This is the Holy Spirit. There is an assumption here that this will be a partnership, not a situation of you making the requests and God doing all the answering. Remember, when you do the possible, and then God will do the impossible.

4. You shouldn't have to suffer

"The thief comes only to steal and kill and destroy; I have come that they may have life, and have it to the full." John 10:10.

This is a glorious verse but it does not mean that God wants you to have an easy life, but rather a purposeful and full life. The bible gives us countless examples of over-comers. If there were no hardships there would be nothing to overcome. I do not think that God wants people to be sick and live horrific lives, but if we take this verse to the extreme, we end up with a cuddly God who is out of control. Heresy is a truth taken to its logical extension.

What we can say confidently is that the enemy has no power, God is in complete control and He is good. We cannot say that God wants life to be rosy all the time, because He does permit bad things to happen both today and throughout scripture. I do not know why there is so much suffering across the world but I do know that God loves the world so much he sent His only son to come and die for it. I know that Jesus came and suffered too and can identify with any amount of pain that we could have. God does want us to have a fantastic life, but experience tells me that sometimes life has its seasons of pain and I do not find that this contradicts anything in scripture. God never promised you an easy life, but he does promise if you trust Him, it will be a full life and you will have His help to overcome anything that comes your way.

5. Your tithes will come back to you, ten fold!

Proverbs 11:24 – "One man gives freely, yet gains even more; another withholds unduly but comes to poverty."

Luke 6:38 – "Give and it will be given to you, a good measure pressed down, shaken together and running over, will be poured into your lap. For with the measure you use, it will be measured to you."

This is a principle but not a promise. Whilst it is true that you reap what you sow; giving to get, is not truly giving. I have heard TV preachers use these verses as a means to manipulate you into handing over your money. There are many great TV evangelists and famous preachers and if you are currently donating to them, fantastic! I would always urge people to give their tithes to their local church first, before any other mega-church. This is your decision of course, but it saddens me to see the local church struggling, while their congregations are tithing to a mega-church at the other side of the world.

When you give, God looks at your heart. It is not good teaching to say that you will definitely get back your tithes plus more. It is possible that our reward will be a spiritual one when we give, not a financial one.

Jesus says,

"When you give a luncheon or dinner, do not invite your friends, your brothers or sisters, your relatives, or your rich neighbours; if you do, they may invite you back and so you will be repaid. But when you give a banquet, invite the poor, the crippled, the lame, the blind, and you will be blessed. Although they cannot repay you, you will be repaid at the resurrection of the righteous." Luke 14:12-14.

If you are tight-fisted and not generous with your money, you will be trapped into a poverty mindset. If you are generous and come from a position of abundance, you will likely have more money come back to you. But this is a principle and not a promise. Give because you want to give and because God has given much to you. Do not give because the preacher said that you will get it back, times ten.

Exercises

1. Write some of the misconceptions you may have had around money.
For example,

Rich people are greedy

You cannot be rich and spiritual

God doesn't want me to be rich

Money is the root of all kinds of evil

Others:

2. Decide, are these beliefs helpful? Are they biblical?

If the answer is no, make a decision to STOP this illogical thinking that will strip you from being an effective and happy person.

3. Explain out loud to yourself, to another person or in a journal, about how your old thinking was wrong and now argue your new position.

CHAPTER 9
Get Financially Free

We have learned about money in the previous chapter and have busted some of the myths around it. We know that money is a great tool and that God smiles upon us while we work hard and smart, to make as much as possible, in the quickest time frame possible, for His glory.

By the age of twenty-one I had achieved financial freedom. I am not talking about being debt free, but financially free, meaning you can retire for life should you want to. In this chapter I will be defining financial freedom and explaining how anybody can achieve it.

Stop trading your time for money

In Robert Kiyosaki's book, Rich Dad Poor Dad, we see how most people work for money, when they should be making money work for them. Money is a terrible master, but a great servant. This is a mind shift for most people as it is something that is not learnt in school. Let me begin by explaining the difference between active and passive income.

Active income is the kind of income we are all familiar with. You work once and get paid once. You are trading your time for money. Passive income is where you work once but get paid indefinitely. So if you have an income of say £3,000 in monthly passive income, you will receive it without doing anything for it. It's automatic.

I am not interested in active income and from the age of seventeen entered into the world of passive income. It completely changed my life. I realised that the goal was not to be rich, but to accumulate passive income. I worked out what I needed to live on, and then set out to earn that figure in passive income.

The formula for financial freedom

The formula for financial freedom is really simple. Work out how much money per month you need to live on, and then build a passive income that covers your monthly expenditures.
So if it costs you £5,000 per month to live on, then work up a monthly passive income of £5,000, and you will be financially free.

Passive Income ≥ Living Expenditures
(Passive Income is equal to or greater than you living expenses).

So the first thing that we will do is work out exactly how much it costs you currently to live. You may already know this, you may need to go through your bank statements. Work this out below:

Utility Bills = £

Car costs = £

Rent / Mortgage payments = £

Gifts = £

Going out = £

Food = £

Tithes / Donations = £

Clothes = £

Travel = £

Emergency = £

Debt payments = £

Other = £

Total: £

(This total amount is the figure of monthly passive income that you need)

The three steps to financial freedom:

The first step to financial freedom is really simple. Some people have become 50% closer to financial freedom when learning this within 24-hours. So get ready...

1. Simplify your expenditures

If you currently need £5,000 per month to survive but you can simplify this to £2,500 then you're 50% closer to your goal of financial freedom. This is known as 'delayed gratification' because you can always increase this figure later, but the priority here is to replace your needed income with passive income. Being financially free does not mean having a flashy lifestyle, it means having the time to focus on what you are called to do.

I told this to a friend back in 2009 and he laughed at me. He said that I was being naive to assume that most people could shrink their expenditures, and he himself was an example of somebody who was already living on an income that was as low as it could possibly be. He explained how it was different for me, because at the time, I was not married. Maybe you can relate to this guy and think he is right? If so, think again. Just a few months later he moved out of the country and had to close his English bank account down. Something happened during this process that I will remember forever. When closing his bank account for good, he was absolutely horrified when seeing all the direct debits that were leaving his account every single month and he had no idea what they even were for. After investigating he found out that for years he had been paying for unwanted magazine subscriptions, a forgotten about gym membership, insurance for out-of-date stuff and my personal favourite, a dating agency subscription despite now being married!

What unnecessary things are you paying for? How low could you shrink your expenditures while you build up your passive income?

2. Manage your money

I heard an incredible money management strategy by T Harv Eker at a conference called Millionaire Mind Intensive. When hearing this, I said to myself,

"I am so going to start doing that."

Did I do it? NO!

The conference was so good that I went back the following year. I heard the same section on money management and knew that this was genius and it would revolutionise my finances. I said to myself,

"Right, this time I am actually going to do it and I can't wait."

I got home, and did I do it? NO!

You can probably guess, I went back again the following year for the third time. I heard this money management principle a final time, but this time I said to myself,

"Yeah, I already know that!"

It was only when Harv said,

"If you are not doing something, then you do not know it!"

Finally, I put this simple process into action and within twelve months I was financially free. It is very simple but extremely effective. Please don't read this without applying it. Also, please don't say, "I know that" if you are not actually doing it.

Pay yourself a wage

The first thing you need to do is pay yourself a wage. If you already have a wage, that is great. If you are self-employed and each month your income varies, sort this out immediately. I speak to so many people who say that their profits are far too varied to pay themselves a wage, but it is actually really easy.

Here is how you do it:
a) Take a look at your income over the last year and from this work out your average monthly income.

b) Take 10% off this average monthly figure, giving you a conservative monthly income.

c) Set up a standing order from your business account to your personal account, on the 1st of each month for this conservative monthly amount.

d) If you cannot afford to live on this monthly amount, earn more!

e) If you earn much over this figure one month, keep it in the pot, because you are sure to have some bad months too.

f) If the pot grows really big, reassess your set monthly income and consider increasing it.

Get six bank accounts

Now that you have a set wage each month, it is time to get six bank accounts set up. This will enable you to manage your money, rather than your money managing you. Each time you get paid you must divide your wage into these six accounts. There are so many levels to why this is genius, but let me tell you what each account should be named and how much should go into each to begin with:

Essentials - 50%
Give - 10%
Play - 10%
Savings - 10%
Investments - 10%
Education - 10%

So if your wage is £2,000, then you put 50% (£1,000) in Essentials and 10% (£200) in each other account. The percentages do not have to be exact. I met a guy called Carl who after hearing this decided to have 90% for Essentials and 2% in each other account. Two years later his finances were fantastic and he even managed to leave his job.

The bible says,

"Whoever can be trusted with very little can also be trusted with much." Luke 16:10.

If God sees you being faithful with the little you have and managing your money well, He will release much more to you.

Let me briefly explain what each account is for:

Essentials (50%)
This is for bare necessities such as rent, mortgage payments, food, car costs and the like.

Give (10%)
This is your tithes and offerings. You can of course give more than this, but 10% is a good starting point. No matter how little you have, do not rob God. Many people tell themselves that they will give once they have more, this is not true. If you will not give now, you never will. Be a cheerful giver but a disciplined one too.

Play (10%)
This is money to be used on luxuries such as massages, fancy dinners and fun days out. You must spend this each and every month. Most arguments in the marriage are about money because one is a spender and the other a saver. If you do this, it will

eliminate your arguments because you will be able to spend lavishly, but it will be a controlled amount. Everybody is a winner! It is forbidden to not spend this each month because it will make you feel rich and you will begin to see life from a position of abundance. The people who are too tight with themselves, usually end up rebelling and splashing out in an uncontrolled way later in life.

Savings (10%)
This is things that you have to save up for. A new car, a holiday or maybe some home improvements.

Investments (10%)
This is money that should never be spent but only invested into things that will generate you a passive income such as property, systemised businesses, vending machines, stocks and shares. As you do this, your income will grow over time and you will be shocked at how fast it snowballs creating financial freedom, without trying. Some ask what they should spend their investment money on though. That is why we also have the Education account.

Education (10%)
The more you learn, the more you earn. The most valuable asset you will ever have is your brain. Invest in yourself, above all. Read books, go to seminars and immerse yourself in personal development.

Further Study

If you need more help with this, I would highly recommend reading 'Secrets of the Millionaire Mind' by T Harv Eker. Also read, 'The Richest Man in Babylon' by George Samuel Clason.

3. Create passive income

The final step to achieving financial freedom is to begin exploring ways to earn passive income. I do not intend to give you an exhaustive list on ways to generate this here, but my advice is to get into property investing. You can make serious passive income very easily in property even without having any money to start with. This is a whole subject in itself but I would highly recommend visiting www.property-investors.co.uk for access to free information about how to get 50% Return on Investments and how to become financially free using property as a vehicle.

Exercises

1. Simplify your expenditures to as low as possible.

Utility Bills = £

Car costs = £

Rent / Mortgage payments = £

Gifts = £

Going out = £

Food = £

Tithes / Donations = £

Clothes = £

Travel = £

Emergency = £

Debt payments = £

Other = £

Total: £

(This total amount is the figure of monthly passive income that you need)

2. Pay yourself a wage and set up six bank accounts in order to manage your money, like the rich.

Essentials - 50%
Give - 10%
Play - 10%
Savings - 10%
Investments - 10%
Education - 10%

3. Learn about property investment at www.property-investors.co.uk and sign up for some free resources.

CHAPTER 10
Run a Good Business

Y ou may not currently run a business but I suggest that you probably do. However, if the world of business is really not what God has called you to do, then in this chapter you can replace the word "business" with "enterprise", "project", "ministry" or even "influence".

We are going to be looking at the book of Acts and learning from how they set up the early church and what systems and principles they put in place. There were four fundamental principles they used and if you follow these same principles today, it will completely revolutionise the effectiveness of your business.

Is the book of Acts really applicable to business? Yes.

The Christian church began with just a dozen or so people. They put into practise these four principles and within just a matter of months it went from around a dozen, to hundreds and hundreds of thousands. Would you like to gain an additional few hundred thousand clients, followers or sterling pounds to your business? The answer is yes. It is recorded in the book of Acts that within a matter of months, the disciples "turned the world upside down". They were highly effective Christians.

Before we explore these four points, do you think it is distasteful taking the early church and the book of Acts, and stealing these principles in order to try and grow our businesses? Is this a little twisted and would Jesus be happy with us doing it? Before you answer that, remember that we cannot separate the secular and the spiritual, because everything is spiritual. The principles that should be applied for the spiritual, are the exact same that should be applied for the practical. It is very easy to have a mindset that says,

"This is spiritual, but this over here, is practical. On one side are the principles for our faith, and the other are the principles for our business."

However, the bible is active and living. It is useful on all accounts and is our manual for life. So, on that basis I do not think that it is distasteful to learn about business from the book of Acts.

So with that in mind, here are the four biblical lessons that will set your business up to flourish.

Four Fundamentals to Running a Good Business

1. Love your product

Before the early Church was established in the book of Acts, comes the book of Matthew, Mark, Luke and John. In these books the disciples are spending time with Jesus and in that time they fall in love with Him. They become so excited about Jesus that by the time that He ascends to heaven and tells them,

"Go and make disciples."

They cannot resist but to go and tell everybody because they love their product and are excited about their message. They go around proclaiming,

"We have got Good News to tell you!"

The product that they are selling is that Jesus is Lord and He has come to forgive their sins. The call to action is, "Will you believe in Him?"

When you tell people about your business and your products, do you feel that you are bringing good news? Do you excitedly say,

"Hey, I have this product and it is fantastic!"

Or do you go into your appointments with no energy and negative feelings about the whole process?

If you love you product, know your product and are passionate about the thing that you are selling, then that is the first step to running a good business.

Just before Jesus ascended to heaven and the disciples would establish the church, it is interesting to note this conversation,

Acts 1:6-8

"Then they gathered around him and asked him, "Lord, are you at this time going to restore the kingdom to Israel?" He said to them: "It is not for you to know the times or dates the Father has set by his own authority. But you will receive power when the Holy Spirit comes on you; and you will be my witnesses in Jerusalem, and in all Judea and Samaria, and to the ends of the earth."

They were asking for all the minor details about timings and future events and Jesus told them it was not important for them to know.

I hear many people getting hung up in business asking many detailed questions and getting distracted. This can be procrastination and an excuse why not to get to work.

For example,

"What if X,Y and Z happens?
Is anybody already doing this though?
Maybe it isn't the right time to start a business?"

Jesus would tell you,

"This is not for you to know right now. But get on and go, and I will be with you."

2. Know your market

This is an interesting one because surely the disciples' message was for everybody. They did not have a niche market did they? Actually, yes.

Matthew wrote his gospel specifically for the Jews. That was his market and whom he was aiming to reach. Mark speaks to the Gentiles. Luke to the Greeks.

This is why there are four different gospels because they are all writing to different people and audiences. They each know their market.

When Jesus tells them to go, he specifically tells them to go to the Jews and Gentiles, starting in Jerusalem, then Judea, then Samaria and finally to the ends of the earth. This was done in an organised way, where they were going to set places with a different marketing approach to different people.

In the same way, you need to know who your market is? Who is your product for? Once you know exactly who your market is, it will make it easier to find people interested.

I have heard many business owners at networking events that stand up and say things like,

"I am a mobile hairdresser and I am looking for new customers. I can help anybody with hair. Who do you know?"

That may sound feasible because this hairdresser can genuinely help anybody with hair, but looking at Acts, they wouldn't have said that. They may have said,

"I am a hairdresser and I am looking specifically to help old ladies in care homes based in the Birmingham area. Who do you know?"

This is much more specific and will be guaranteed to be more effective. A vague market will lead to vague results.

Matthew would speak to the Jews and preach the law perfectly to them and raise the standards of 'good' to a whole new level. This is because they thought that they were already good enough to get to heaven. When they would finally realise they needed a Saviour, he would tell them the Good News. Mark had the same ultimate message, but his market was the Greeks and he had a completely different approach. In the same way, decide exactly who you are marketing to and who your product or service is for.

3. Find your market

Now you know exactly who your market is, next, you need to know where to find these people. Where are your prospective customers? Where do they live? Where do they shop? Where do they network?

If you are selling luxury cars to middle-aged rich men, you would probably find them in golf clubs. If your business is around health products, your market will probably be in gyms.

The early church disciples loved their product, knew their market and knew where to find their market. You may think I am taking this way to an extreme. Jesus really had not thought it through like this and was not running his ministry like a business. Jesus was like a hippie and just wandered around aimlessly and the Holy Spirit would chaotically send him to random places with no ambition or plan, right? No!

Luke 10

Verse 1
"After this the Lord appointed seventy-two others and sent them two by two ahead of him to every town and place where he was about to go."

It is clear that Jesus knew exactly where he was going ahead of time, and strategically sent others in a particular order to go before him. Jesus was a manager and a strategist.

Verse 2a
"The harvest is plentiful, but the workers are few."

Jesus knew that he had a massive market ready to hear the good news. He just needed people to get the message out there.

Verse 2b
"Ask the Lord of the harvest, therefore, to send out workers into his harvest field. Go! I am sending you out like lambs among wolves."

Some Christians say that business is a dark place, but Jesus calls us to be lambs among wolves, to be light in the darkness. Interesting to note that we are told to ask for Gods help. We are in partnership with the Lord God Almighty.

Verse 4
"Do not take a purse or bag or sandals; and do not greet anyone on the road."

Was Jesus being miserable and unfriendly here? No. They had business to take care of and Jesus was preventing them from procrastinating. When you are on a mission and people stop to chat, it is perfectly ok to say,

"Sorry, I cannot talk right now."

Don't feel the need to come up with long excuses, just keep walking. I would rather upset a few people at times, but be highly effective, than have everybody like me, but be ineffective. You are called to leave an eternal legacy, not to be liked.

It is good to have protected time within your business. This is when you are focusing on one mission and turn all distractions off. When I am in protected time, even the Queen of England would not be able to get hold of me because my calls are diverted and I will not greet anybody on the road. If Jesus had been speaking today, he may have said,

"Do not take your iPad and do not pass any shops; if your mobile phone rings, ignore it."

Verse 6-11
"When you enter a house, first say, 'Peace to this house.' If someone who promotes peace is there, your peace will rest on them; if not, it will return to you. Stay there, eating and drinking whatever they give you, for the worker deserves his wages. Do not move around from house to house. "When you enter a town and are welcomed, eat what is offered to you. Heal the sick who are there and tell them, 'The kingdom of God has come near to you.' But when you enter a town and are not welcomed, go into its streets and say, 'Even the dust of your town we wipe from our feet as a warning to you. Yet be sure of this: The kingdom of God has come near.'"

There is an old saying that says,

"Some will, some won't, so what? Next!"

I spoke to a new business lady and asked her how many customers she had. She responded,

"I am working on three at the moment."

She explained that there were a few lined up but they needed a little more persuasion before they would buy. They had been coming up with excuses for some months now and were currently avoiding her calls.
I told her that she needed to move on and get herself in front of more people. One of my business mentors told me that his three secrets to success were,

"1.See more people. 2.See more people. 3.See more people."

Jesus was giving strategic instructions in a particular area and they were to do exactly that. Go into a house and if the prospect had not bought into the idea within a few seconds, move on to the next house.

Jesus knew where his market was and sent his distributors out to spread the message in a deliberate way. His distributors being those who were part of distributing the good news.

4. What to say?

Lastly, and possibly most importantly, what do we say?

Once you are in front of your market, how do you seal the deal? Of course, this depends on your business but my advice would be to practise what you have to say.

a) Have a sentence prepared when people ask, "What do you do?"

b) Have a 60 second elevator pitch prepared when people ask for more details.

c) Have a five-minute explanation of your business ready.

d) Have a twenty-minute full presentation of your Unique Sales Proposition.

When I first set up Training Kings, I was in a meeting with my bank manager. She asked me what I did and I told her that I ran a Christian Business Network, Training Kings. She seemed excited as she was a Christian and asked me what that entailed. We were sat over a coffee and I was under no time pressure. She was expectantly waiting for some insight but I was lost for words. I just didn't know where to start and had not thought through how to explain it. This would have been a perfect opportunity for the 60-second elevator pitch but I blew my chance and possibly lost a great member of Training Kings, due to my lack of practise.

You never know when you may have a twenty-minute opportunity to share to a group and you need to be ready and have rehearsed it.

The disciples were mostly young, inexperienced and uneducated men, yet they had practised and memorised their scripts. Peter was known to be a brash fisherman yet look at Acts 2 and you will see how much scripture he could quote off by heart. He begins by addressing his audience, his market,

"Fellow Jews and all of you who live in Jerusalem, let me explain this to you; listen carefully to what I say." Acts 2:14

He then goes on to quote a long piece of powerful scripture and give a well prepared speech. Towards the end he finishes with his call to action,

"Repent and be baptised, every one of you, in the name of Jesus Christ for the forgiveness of your sins. And you will receive the gift of the Holy Spirit. The promise is for you and your children and for all who are far off—for all whom the Lord our God will call." (Acts 2:38-40).

How many people bought into the vision and became followers of Jesus from that speech? About three thousand!

Imagine if you had crafted and memorised your business scripts so when people ask you questions about your product and services you could respond confidently without stumbling or waffling. This would have a massive positive effect on your business.

Conclusion

The four fundamentals that the early church used to grow so fast were that they loved their product, they knew their market, they knew where to find their market and they knew exactly what to say.

I will close this chapter with Stephen, who is one of my biblical heroes from the book of Acts. Stephen was preaching the gospel and spreading the Good News of Jesus when religious leaders who hated him, encircled him and picked up stones ready to kill him.

Stephen knew they were about to kill him and had a few options.

1. Run!
2. Reason with them.
3. Explain his message quickly before being stoned

Stephen chose none of these options. He decided as he was about to die, it was time for him to recite his full twenty minute Unique Sales Presentation. Stephen could have probably got away but he was so in love with his product, Jesus, that he could not resist but preach the truth even if that meant dying for it.

Stephen recited his twenty-minute pitch that was around 1,300 words long, before being stoned to death. Although it was recorded that he fell asleep, because we know that as Christians we do not die but simply fall asleep and wake up in the arms of Jesus.

Stephen loved his product so much that he would die for it, as did all of the other disciples.

I am not saying that you should die for your product, but I am saying that we serve a God who is so good that He is worth dying for. If your faith is not worth dying for, then perhaps you need to go back to fundamental number 1 and love your product. I guarantee that if you spend time reading about Jesus in scripture and talking to Him in prayer, you will fall in love more and more with Jesus. This is the best thing I ever did. So yes, grow your business and strategically expand, but never forget your first love, and keep Christ on the throne and in His rightful place.

Exercises

1. Precisely what is your business, product, ministry or vision plan?

2. Do you love it? If not, find something else and go back to exercise number 1.

3. Who specifically is your market?

4. Create a script to explain and promote your business.

- Have a sentence prepared when people ask, "What do you do?"

- 60 Second Elevator Pitch

- Five Minute Business Explanation

- Twenty Minute Full Presentation

5. Is your faith more important than your business? If no, spend time with Jesus and let yourself develop a love for Him like you were created to do.

CHAPTER 11
Join a Network

Friends

There is an African proverb that says,

"If you want to go fast, go alone. If you want to go far, go together."

I know that you have a pioneer's heart and desire to leave a legacy otherwise you would not have got so far in reading this book. The cancer that could now potentially rob your hopes and dreams is isolation. Isolation is the biggest killer there is, and it will prevent you from achieving great things. In order to make a difference we need to have people around us believing in the vision. Many people say that they need more finance when actually that is not the problem, they need more friends. Friends are those people who know all about you and still like you. I completely agree with Pastor Gary Spicer who believes that,

"Friends bring favour."

Surround yourself with positive people who want the best for you and will stand with you in the vision. Not everybody has to agree with you on everything, but they do need to have the same spirit that you have, namely, a Kingdom spirit. Friends will encourage you through the storms and cheer you on through the trails. When you are not thinking clearly, they will guide you. When you have blind spots, they will see to it.

"As iron sharpens iron, so a friend sharpens a friend." Proverbs 27:17.

Enemies

There will be people who you think are your friends but actually want to see you fail. I have been let down, slandered and stabbed in the back by many 'friends' and have seen the joy in their eyes during my downfalls. If not already, this will happen to you. Every pioneer should expect this as it happened to Jesus, the pioneer of pioneers. Don't sign up for the class that spends hours wondering why this happens, it just does. Move on towards the goal and fix your eyes on Jesus. Do not become disillusioned with people or lose hope. As Jim Rohn humorously says,

"There are only nine nasty people in the world . . . they just move around an awful lot."

You need to learn to be soft hearted but thick skinned. The bible tells us to be "as wise as serpents, but as innocent as doves." Matthew 10:16.

After King Saul had repeatedly tried to kill David, David forgave him and even spared Saul's life. This led Saul to be remorseful and he asked David if things could go back to be the way they were. David forgave Saul, but he would not go back to his house.

"Then Saul returned home, but David and his men went up to the stronghold." 1 Samuel 24:22.

If you are bitter towards those who do you wrong, it will only hold you back and make you ineffective. Forgive them as Christ forgives you, but still be as wise as a serpent and protect your vision.

Business Networking

Jesus started his business networking at the age of twelve. His parents lost him and found him networking and asking questions in the temple. Jesus was getting on with his Heavenly Father's business as he grew in wisdom and stature, and in favour with God and man.

My property business that grew so fast that by the age of twenty-one I could have retired for life, came as a result of who I knew, not what I knew. This happened through business networking.

Robert Kiyosaki says,

"Most people look for work. Rich (effective) people look for networks."

I realised that most businesses failed due to the lack of business they were bringing in. I saw many people who had a fantastic product or service but struggled because nobody knew about it. The usual way to get more business is to advertise. However, I grew my business from scratch without spending a penny on advertising.

Business networking can and will replace expensive advertising. This is the case for limited companies, sole traders, churches, charities and just about any organisation in the world. If you need to raise awareness in order to grow, you need to be business networking. If you have not got a project, then maybe you need to go and get one.

Fiona was working full-time in a dead end job, but had a business on the side that had precisely zero customers. She was shy about her business and although she had business cards and a website, it was really just a dream for her and she didn't have the time to do much with it because of her job, church and family commitments.

Fiona came along to a Christian business-networking event, Training Kings. She was overwhelmed by the buzzing energy in the room and inspired by the speeches. It came to the dreaded time for her to have to stand up and explain in 60 seconds about what she did and what help specifically she was looking for. Fiona nervously explained that she had this little business and was looking for support and some customers. That morning over breakfast she was passed four fantastic connections as well as somebody that wanted to sign up as a customer right away.

Of course, Fiona came back and began to get more and more business. She also grew as a person and made some genuine friends. Within less than one year she was earning more in her part-time business than she did at her full-time job. Fiona has now quit her job and works full-time on her business and has become much more effective in her church too. Each month her dreams get bigger and it has been a joy to see her grow. Fiona is one of many people who have had their lives changed through business networking.

When networking, just make sure that you use "the ant philosophy" from chapter 5. Go to give, not to get. As you pass business to other members and help them, they will naturally want to help you back. This is not 'giving to get' but more about sowing and reaping. When you sow into others and into a network, you will most certainly, later reap.

Do not dish out business cards and verbally vomit your vision over everybody, but ask others about their projects and be interested. Listen and try to help. The reward will be far greater and you will learn more too. If you are nervous about this whole process, feel the fear and do it anyway. People who network are used to welcoming new people and you will enjoy it a lot more than you expect. Most people overestimate how clever others are and underestimate their own intelligence and value. Go with confidence and be completely genuine. The best thing about you is you.

Exercises

Find a Christian Business Network and book on. If there is none, then just find a regular business network.

www.trainingkings.co.uk

CHAPTER 12
Live for Eternity

Build Riches in Heaven

Last year, my wife and I had to go to Zambia on a mission trip. We decided to go a couple of weeks early so that we could spend some quality time together at the Victoria Falls in Zimbabwe. Amanda, my wife, loves shopping. She could spend a whole day going from shop to shop buying things that we would probably never see again. I had to stress to her that we had zero space left in the cases so there would be no way we could take anything home with us. This had to be a trip where we would just enjoy the moment because anything purchased for later, would be binned at the airport.

If Amanda had spent all of her time on this trip shopping, and had bought an endless list of clothes, accessories, ornaments and souvenirs; what would you think? You would think that she was being foolish. Why? Because she would only be able to hold onto those items for a maximum of a few weeks and then it would have to be left at the airport.

In the same way, life is extremely short and when we die, we will take nothing with us to heaven.

"For we brought nothing into the world, and we can take nothing out of it." 1 Timothy 6:7.

When I see people building businesses in order to accumulate a large net worth to sit on, but have no sense of eternity, it makes me sad. This earth, as we know it, is just a glimpse of our eternity. It is insane how we spend so much time worrying about such a tiny piece of the cake.

"You do not even know what will happen tomorrow. What is your life? You are a mist that appears for a little while and then vanishes." James 4:14.

There is nothing wrong with building up a good life on earth, but if you spend more time planning life on earth than life in heaven, you need to get your priorities right. Jesus says,

"Do not store up for yourselves treasures on earth, where moths and vermin destroy, and where thieves break in and steal. But store up for yourselves, treasures in heaven where moths and vermin do not destroy, and where thieves do not break in and steal. For where your treasure is, there your heart will be also." Matthew 6:19-21.

Imagine if there was a dying man on the side of the road and the ambulance came, only to start cleaning his trousers and sewing his shirt back up. This would be outrageous. If they were to repair his body first and make sure he is fit and healthy, then it would be fine to fix his clothes up.

In the same way, there is nothing wrong with buying a nice house on earth and creating a wealthy lifestyle. The problem comes when you have not even sorted your place out in heaven or even thought about the eternal riches, but are obsessed with earthly riches.

What are Heavenly Riches?

Heavenly riches are things that are eternal. We often hear people talking about eternal riches, but what does that actually mean?

Well to sow into eternal things, is to sow into people. People are eternal and every human being in the world, will never cease to exist because we are all made in the image of God.

"God created mankind in his own image, in the image of God he created them; male and female." Genesis 1:27.

It is impossible to get our heads around eternity because all we have ever known is time. God invented the concept of time. After giving myself a headache trying to comprehend how God has always existed and how we have no end, I have now given up trying, and have decided to study other things instead.

"He has also set eternity in the human heart; yet no one can fathom what God has done from beginning to end." Ecclesiastes 3:11.

Instead of spending time trying to understand eternity, I now spend time trying to understand how I can sow into eternity. This is the question that God will ask us to account for. My conclusion is that building eternal riches happens when you have an eternal impact on another persons life. This may be because you have inspired them, made them feel loved or built them up in some way. Jesus spent his time sowing into peoples lives and awakening them to think eternally.

It is also important to make sure that you, yourself, are built up. It is nearly impossible to leave a positive impact on others while you are in a negative state.

God has called us to live in a cycle of love. We acknowledge God's love for us, which then enables us to love others likewise. When we love others, they see Christ in us and find God themselves. The process continues. It may sound like I am being fluffy and not scriptural but the greatest commandment is to love God and love others.

"We love because he first loved us." 1 John 4:19.

The greatest way you can leave a legacy and have an eternal purpose is by loving God and loving people. This may result in you building some large enterprises here on earth too, but the thing you are actually building is people that are entering into God's eternal Kingdom.

Everything you say has a consequence

There is an old saying,

"Sticks and stones may break my bones, but words will never hurt me."

As Christians, we know that this is not strictly true. In order to leave a legacy, you must be extremely conscious of your words. When Paul wrote to the churches, do you think he knew that his words would be read by millions of people, over two thousand years later?
He probably did not. It is possible that your words will also be remembered years after you have gone.

According to James, your tongue is an extremely powerful force.

James 3:5-8
"The tongue is a small part of the body, but it makes great boasts. Consider what a great forest is set on fire by a small spark. The tongue also is a fire, a world of evil among the parts of the body. It corrupts the whole body, sets the whole course of one's life on fire, and is itself set on fire by hell. All kinds of animals, birds, reptiles and sea creatures are being tamed and have been tamed by mankind, but no human being can tame the tongue. It is a restless evil, full of deadly poison."

There is a time to use harsh words, Jesus did on several occasions, but your goal should always be to build people up. If somebody is being destructive, you may need to shut them down, but this is ultimately for the saving of many lives.

What will heaven be like?

I used to get nauseous thinking about eternity. I hated the idea of having no end and would just envision singing endless worship songs while floating on clouds. This sounded deathly boring to me, but that is not what heaven will be like. Let's look at what the bible says,

"He will wipe every tear from their eyes. There will be no more death or mourning or crying or pain, for the old order of things has passed away." Revelation 21:4.

This includes the pain of boredom. It sounds like a fantasy that there could be no physical or emotional pain whatsoever, but this is what God says in His inspired, preserved Word.

Everything that is good about earth will be magnified in heaven. All your thirsts and desires will be quenched to the extreme. It took God six days to create earth and the universe, but He spent much more time creating heaven. Jesus has personally prepared a place for you.

"In my Father's house are many rooms. If it were not so, would I have told you that I go to prepare a place for you? And if I go and prepare a place for you, I will come again and will take you to myself, that where I am you may be also." John 14:2-3.

When you do fall asleep and wake up in your new eternal home, there will be old friends, angels and The Lord God Himself, waiting to give you a rich welcome.

"Make every effort to confirm your calling and election. For if you do these things, you will never stumble, and you will receive a rich welcome into the eternal kingdom of our Lord and Saviour Jesus Christ." 2 Peter 1:10,11.

I could talk much more, but I would encourage you to continue your own studies on heaven. In a nutshell, it will be awesome!

I used to worry that God would prepare something that He assumed I would like, but in actual fact would not be of my taste, but it is important to remember that God knows you better than you know yourself. All your desires, God gave you in the first place.

Eternal Life Begins Now

When you are a Christian in a relationship with Jesus, eternal life does not begin when you die, it begins now. Many Christians make death their Saviour, when Jesus is actually their Saviour. Although there will always be troubles and suffering in the world, until Jesus returns, we are citizens of heaven and can enjoy eternal life now. We are pre-wired to be happy, effective, successful and can live "on earth as in heaven".

Eternal life is being connected to God, who is eternal. I pray you enjoy Him now and forever, and in doing so will also glorify Him.

Amen!

Exercises

1. What will prevent you from being short sighted and forgetting about eternity?

2. How will you build treasures in heaven?

3. How can you better reflect God's eternal love to your family and within your work?

Now put these into practise and leave an eternal legacy.

Final Words

It has been extremely rewarding for me to write this book and I hope you have had a similar experience reading as I have had in writing.

In conclusion, I urge you to continue developing your love for God and love for people. As you do this, find a worthwhile cause that you can dedicate your life to that is fitting with your God-given strengths. Expect opposition and hardships, but press on with all your might and as you partner with God, expect miracles to happen. Join a Christian business network and surround yourself with good people who believe in your mission. Learn about money and use this as a tool along the way, but ensure that the main thing stays the main thing, and never stop building treasure in heaven.

I hope to meet you in person if we have not met yet. You can see my schedule online at www.samuelleeds.org

Yours in His Service

Samuel Leeds

About The Author

Samuel Leeds is an international speaker and an accomplished businessperson. His mission is to inspire and equip Christians to be highly effective for the Kingdom.

Samuel became a Christian at seventeen years old and spent three years at Birmingham Bible Institute training for ministry and studying theology. Since then he established Good News All Round which is a charity that brings clean water to third world countries in Africa as well as bringing the good news of Jesus.

With the help of business mentors and the use of biblical financial wisdom, Samuel built up a property portfolio in his early 20's enabling him to become financially free. He is extremely passionate about teaching money management within the church amongst many other topics.

He founded Training Kings, which is currently that largest Christian business network in the UK, and has had the privilege to speak at conference and churches worldwide.

He and his wife, Amanda, live in the West Midlands, England.

Printed in Great Britain
by Amazon